How to use this book

Follow the advice, in italics, given for you on each page.
Support the children as they read the text that is shaded in cream.
***Praise** the children at every step!*

Detailed guidance is provided in the Read Write Inc. Phonics Handbook.

8 reading activities

Children:

- *Practise reading the speed sounds.*
- *Read the green, red and challenge words for the story.*
- *Listen as you read the introduction.*
- *Discuss the vocabulary check with you.*
- *Read the story.*
- *Re-read the story and discuss the 'questions to talk about'.*
- *Re-read the story with fluency and expression.*
- *Practise reading the speed words.*

Speed sounds

Consonants *Say the pure sounds (do not add 'uh').*

f ff	l ll	m	n	r	s ss	v ve	z zz s	sh	th	ng nk

b bb	c k ck	d	g gg	h	j	p	qu	t	w wh	x	y	ch tch

Vowels *Say the vowel sound and then the word, eg 'a', 'at'.*

at	hen	in	on	up	day	see	high	blow	zoo

*Each box contains one sound but sometimes more than one grapheme. Focus graphemes are **circled**.*

Green words

Read in Fred Talk (pure sounds).

sand rich off deck smash ship lock chest stiff

Read in syllables.

frog' man → frogman

Read the root word first and then with the ending.

lift → lifts ring → rings drop → drops

Red words

the I of to

Vocabulary check

Discuss the meaning (as used in the story) after the children have read the word.

	definition:
frogman	*a diver, with flippers and special equipment to help him breathe under water*
octopus	*a sea creature with eight arms*
chest	*a big, strong box*
deck	*the name used for the floor on a ship*

Punctuation to note in this story:

Fred	*Capital letters for names*
The Bash	*Capital letters that start sentences*
.	*Full stop at the end of each sentence*
!	*Exclamation mark used to show surprise*

The chest in the sand

Introduction

Have you ever seen a diver? They wear wetsuits and swim under water looking at interesting creatures and objects.

Frogman Fred is a diver who finds a pirate's treasure chest buried in the sand. He's very excited as he thinks about what might be inside! But Fred is in for a big surprise. Let's see what happens.

Story written by Cynthia Rider
Illustrated by Tim Archbold

Frogman Fred spots a chest in the sand.

I bet it's full of rings and rich things.

Fred pulls the chest on to the deck of his ship.

The lid of the chest is stuck
and the lock is stiff.

Fred hits the lock. *Bash! Smash!*
The lock drops off.

Fred lifts up the lid. *And up pops …*

... a big octopus!

Questions to talk about

FIND IT QUESTIONS

- ✓ *Turn to the page*
- ✓ *Read the question to the children*
- ✓ *Find the answer*

Page 8: *Who spots the chest in the sand?*

Page 9: *What does Fred think is in the chest?*

Page 10: *Where does Fred take the chest?*

Page 11: *Why is the chest difficult to open?*

Page 12: *How does Fred open the chest?*

Page 13: *What is really in the chest?*
What do you think Fred feels? (shocked/disappointed/angry)